A Quiet Voice
Growing Loud

A Quiet Voice Growing Loud

Poetic Reflections on Healing, Identity, and Loss

Kimberly Carpel Damessous

RESOURCE *Publications* · Eugene, Oregon

A QUIET VOICE GROWING LOUD
Poetic Reflections on Healing, Identity, and Loss

Copyright © 2025 Kimberly Carpel Damessous. All rights reserved. Except for brief quotations in critical publications or reviews, no part of this book may be reproduced in any manner without prior written permission from the publisher. Write: Permissions, Wipf and Stock Publishers, 199 W. 8th Ave., Suite 3, Eugene, OR 97401.

Resource Publications
An Imprint of Wipf and Stock Publishers
199 W. 8th Ave., Suite 3
Eugene, OR 97401

www.wipfandstock.com

PAPERBACK ISBN: 979-8-3852-4953-4
HARDCOVER ISBN: 979-8-3852-4954-1
EBOOK ISBN: 979-8-3852-4955-8
VERSION NUMBER 07/24/25

To Lee—
my steadfast heart, my quiet strength,
your love holds everything steady.

And to Alana, Sebastian, Claire, and Julia—
brilliant sparks in my sky,
you color my world with wonder.
Each of you, I love like no other.

To my Creator, thank you for being
the strength beneath my voice.

Because of you all, I write
and found the courage to share my voice with the world.
With all my love, always.

Contents

Introduction | ix

I Buried My Dad Today | 1
Daydreaming of Heaven | 2
Black Canvas | 3
I Want to Be Free | 5
Parenthood | 6
Silent Voices | 7
Lovers' Song | 8
Tick Tock, Tick Tock | 9
Who Is to Say | 10
Searching | 11
New Beginnings | 12
Mental Warfare | 13
Morning's Hour | 15
Wretched Sting | 16
Country Living | 17
Tweet Tweet | 18
When Strings Come Undone | 20
New Politics | 21
Imagination | 22

Conflicted | 23
Safety | 25
Confusion | 26
Brighter Days | 27
Wish You Could See Me | 28
New Year | 29
I Am a Wanderer | 30
Sinking | 31
Virgin | 32
Where Is Her Honor? | 34
Dreaming | 36
Lost | 37
Holiday Cheer | 38
Familial Pain | 39
Fearful | 41
Woman | 42
Windy Day | 43
Running | 44
Afloat | 46
Thankful | 47

Index | 49

Introduction

We all experience the world in our own unique ways. My journey to capture that experience in poetry form perhaps began the moment I read Elizabeth Barrett Browning's "How Do I Love Thee?" followed by Maya Angelou's "Caged Bird." As a reserved young woman, I discovered that life could be expressed through similes and metaphors—softened and strengthened by imagination. What you hold in your hands is a reflection of my personal journey over the years—an unfolding of life as I experienced it, from being an immigrant child to an evolving young woman in America. Like you, I've faced uncertainty, loss, family conflict, healing, and everything in between.

For years, I simply wrote to understand. Then one day, I realized these words—honest and reflective—might be worth sharing. Maybe, just maybe, they could reach someone else. My hope is that the quiet, young girl who once found her voice through Browning and Angelou might now help you find yours. Or, at the very least, remind you that you are not alone. The very experiences that often make us feel isolated are the ones that connect us most deeply. May these words speak to your soul.

With love,
Kimberly

I Buried My Dad Today

I buried my dad today
Why does life have to be this way?
It still feels so strange to say
but I buried my dad today
I wish there was another way

Everyone's trying to find the right words to say
but nothing they say can take this pain away
Knowing he's no longer in pain does not seem to sway
this pain that I feel inside to be any other way
His name is on my speed dial but he can longer ever say:
Hello or goodbye or how are you today?

Life has a way of moving on, and we're just expected to continue on
as if this did not happen today
Six feet under they put him in the ground
There's an eery ending there that just grips your heart
Knowing that his body is now in the ground
Spirit is gone, and now the body too

I buried my dad today and everything just keeps going on the same
But for me, life is different
A piece of my heart taken, gone
Here I am trying to keep the melancholy away
The children are laughing and screaming, begging me to play
But I buried my dad today
I wish there was another way.

Daydreaming of Heaven

I had a dream the stars were aligned
Your fingertips touched mine and light surrounded me
Tenderly woven, you placed me in your arms
Guarded and shielded from life's shallow streams

Love so pure, its deeds well-read
No guessing game here, no spoilers ahead
Simple and true, love became me
Enveloped in goodness, no eyes have ever seen
Completion at work, I twirled and I twirled

A younger me rose up
Hidden for so long; it burst out quite loudly
Freedom at last, unconstrained, unsuspected
It amused me the same
Oh, how I had forgotten
the sweet joys that made me who I am today

Then the dream went away, as quickly as it came
Oh, life so tragic, if only it would stay.

Black Canvas

All they see is poverty in a generation
that never ceases to master in folly
A continuous whirlwind in the streets
that equals a wide-screen view
Front-page read, for all these faces to see
To mock in contempt and ridicule
Calling my people barbaric animals;
A wasted generation.

But this generation is a part of me that I cannot erase
My brothers and sisters stitched to my hamstrings
with more than just an iron needle and fickle thread.

All they see in their sight is the animosity
that is blaring from the streets with black features
Head wraps and troubled minds
Empty mouths with empty words
Nothing to feed.

All they view is this rampant abhorrence
coming from the mouths of my people
Replicating the actions made in the past

I have a wristwatch that I fumble with
that captures the lies portrayed and accepted by the youth;
We are not better than the streets and scars printed on our backs
Breathe heavy, eyes weary
All I see is the emptiness of black canvas.

Paint on me, forgive the carelessness of empty words
that seem to uplift with wicked hope
and I'll dream of black faces
I'll dream of my people and see their beauty today
as a hope for tomorrow.
And all I see is a black smile, black eyes, and black strength
The silent kind seen only by a kin.

Come closer black canvas and let me paint on you
Stories of a higher generation, ceasing from a wasted population
Surpassing sentences of 25, 35, 45 years to life.
Breathe easy, black canvas
You are better than the media's portrayal
of the wasted population.

I Want to Be Free

I see the trees: they dance in the rain
Swinging hips, linking arms, and shouting real loud
Oh, how I want to be like these trees,
mane swinging with the wind, so delicate and free

How I long to roar like the wind, uninhibited
Yes, just me.
The rain comes pouring and I lift up my face
to taste the sweet drink of peace falling on me

Sweet nature, just take me. Take me in your arms.
I want to fly like the bird! High in the sky
To witness the beauty from way up high
and feel the sweet kisses of the midnight sky

Surrounded by starlight shining so bright.
Oh how I long to be free. Free all night long.

Parenthood

Pretty eyes calling out to me.
Hungry mouths looking for a treat
Fumbling hands searching within reach
for something to touch, something to itch.

Eyes glistering softly
Smiling faces giggling in the corners
All day delight
Small fingers, small toes, but such heavy footing
running swiftly to and fro

Nonstop movement, dizzy, we feel
Yet laughter escapes as we watch in amazement;
The beginning of life just 3 feet tall

Rugged and handsome, debonair
Feisty, sweet, all she can be
Awestruck we stand, hand in hand
taking it all in.

Silent Voices

Earth-shattering lies coated with hatred
Invisible to the eye, they call it self-hatred

But clear in the spirit, the deepest pits of the soul
passed down like rabbits flourishing wild

Who can see it but an inquiring eye
The deepest of minds bypass it like snow
It's right in front of us but no one can know

Shall I call it out
or remain silent real low

Earth-shattering lies coated with hatred
I see it, I do. But does my voice even matter?
Quiet lies, shouted as true
While my voice remains quiet, muffled, it's true.

Lovers' Song

He smells her perfume engulfed in its scent
He lingers a while longer, seeping it in

She knows her power, harvested within
A smile only it takes to reel him right in

A look here, a turn there
It's a game of hide and seek;
Come find me right there
Come find me right here

They chuckle a while longer; they know it must end
Lovers' quarrel only stay for a time
And ending must come, beginnings alike
Let's say goodbye and savor the night

Maybe we'll meet again
This, only fate can tell.

Tick Tock, Tick Tock

Shall I debate
or let it go
Power down
or follow through
The best up ahead
set up for a trap
calling my name,
tick tock tick tock
Time is running.
My feet are sliding
Losing grip,
reality is morphing
My mind is in shambles
My anxiety dreading
Hush hush
deep breath
Be calm, don't show
No weakness
no quarrel
Rest, rest
they'll know.

Who Is to Say

Who is to say that the trees don't speak.
That they do not yell when the leaves fall or bruise
when the storm comes
or the lightening strikes
Who is to say that the trees don't laugh
when the flowers bloom and the landing bird nests its young
Who is the say that the trees don't yell
when the storm wind blows and the planes fly by
Who is to say that the trees don't cry
when the children leave the old treehouse behind
Indeed who is to say that the things we don't see
aren't truly there or that the trees do not speak at all.

Searching

Black bodies, black faces
A million different races
Where I fit? I don't know
Separated by spaces

Far and wide, high and low
I pick up my feet ready to go

Destination unknown but there I will go
To find my people scattered below
I know who I am
Despite it all I know
My blood runs thick, history shows.

New Beginnings

Glorious storm and thunderous rain
I feel its power; its beauty within
Thundering down, calling my name

Clouded and moody wetting terrain
Lightning gleaming with thunder roaring
A storm is coming so time for preparing

Watering the crop and flooring the ground
It's all renewing, mind alike
Streets are empty
Homes abound
finding shelter
Waiting it out
till the rainbow comes flowing
High in the sky
Telling us it's over
New day to come.

Mental Warfare

Bomb them
before they bomb us.
Defense,
attack,
war is coming
It's us versus them.
We're right and they're wrong.
Child's play in action
Yet the masses follow.

They fight for the cause
Scream it in the streets
With little reservation,
they propagate the message
They sell it, justify its misdeeds
Mystify its fruits.
All the while, truth remains hidden
While cowards stay in power.

It's time for us to fight
It's time for us to win
Win an endless battle,
an ultimate war
The victims silenced,
hidden and afraid
While the men in big houses
Slaughter away

Using sons and daughters,
no one can know
They fight for decency
but in reality it's a mask
for such great travesty.
How easy it is to gather the flock
And simply say go.

Morning's Hour

Silent morning with rhythmic breathing
Day's beginning
Soon time for dressing

Shirts and hats for weather's cooling
Get to rising; chicks are waiting

Dog is hungry but quit pestering
Children crying ready for feeding

Momma's tired and not quite waking
Daddy's ready fixing us some eating

Morning glory family gathering
Brand new day; let's get going.

Wretched Sting

Death oh wretched sting
Smothering the deepest pits of my soul
Gnashing the flesh,
leaving but dim light at evening's dusk

Be it not for the pervasiveness of hope within,
what of me would it leave whole?

Country Living

Cluck cluck, they say
Waddle waddle, they sway
Squat squat, they lay
Happy hens, happy day

Sun gleaming with children cheering
Grab a feather for such good weather
War forgotten, it's all daydreaming
Look up high, see those birds flying?

Man in the clouds
Ladies go dancing
Trees swaying hips
Wind starts whistling
Country living in sweet fresh air
Simple life; if you dare.

Tweet Tweet

Tweet this,
tweet that
Don't stop,
won't stop,
never stop.

Information is flowing
and people are wilding
It's a new age
with everyday commentary
Everybody gotta speak,
gotta have a say

My voice over millions
Loud noises, loud laughter,
and anger rising
Defenses are striking,
offenses reacting
From high to low,
night and day
Don't stop,
won't stop,
never stop

Say your piece
and fight the good fight
Shut them down
and build them up

Laugh it up
It's all good fun
Mock him. Shame her
Unite and divide

Don't stop,
never stop
Information is flowing
and people are wilding.

When Strings Come Undone

Mellow hearts combined in one
bring together peace
when the strings come undone.
For healing's most powerful currency
produces far more value
than what the eye can definitively see.

Yet it is hard to see that war is fought by kindness
Though love makes all things right
the greatest language of all is displayed
through selfless love
The kindness of a stranger
speaks volumes to another.
Mellow hearts combine in one
can make miracles happen
when the strings come undone.

New Politics

Confess, confess.
Come forward; repent.
No mercy.
No peace.
Judgment must stand.

Full mouths with many words
Little worth of idle talk
Nonsensical speech that is evasive to boot

Embarrassing and brute
Meant to skew
Expanding confusion
No leader.
No peace.

A mirage and smokescreen
Foggy views and skewed eyesight
Toddlers dressed in suits
Mocking and pointing

Identity hidden and the clowns are laughing
Audience is gripping with their foreheads sweating
No end in sight while the fools keep on playing.
No mercy.
No peace.
A show for all to see.

Imagination

Everybody sleeps
But not everybody remembers to dream
For to dream is to set time still
Escape reality and allow imagination to live.

Conflicted

How do you deal with the dark thoughts,
the ones that grip you, no reconciliation in sight?
Do you run away and hide
or face the giant head-on with fright?

Dog-eat-dog world they say
Not fit for someone like me
Only God understands me because He created me

Where do I fit Lord in a world like this?
Where I'm easily forgotten, replaced with quick speed.

Sinking ocean and sinking sea,
do I really care what they think of me?

My heart on my sleeve
for everyone else to see.
No one can know me,
understand how I speak

Quiet and gentle, roaring and loud
all a part of me but not quite allowed

I am conflicted, feeling alone
nowhere to hide and nowhere to heal
A wounded dog trapped in a fence
where no one can save me.

I just want to be free
Free from the chains they wrapped around me
Free of the labels, the judgments that bind me
I'm not what they want
not what they need
An eternal being where heaven's my home.

With strength, I will fight.
Fight for the ones I love
for the ones like me who need more than this.

Safety

Morning woes do wash over me
Sacred words fill me with a calming breeze
Birds of prey, pass me over
I want to be covered,
wrapped with wonder.

Confusion

I wonder I wonder
When will my days be outnumbered
When will my ways be dismayed
By these continuous days of frequent lies
living life without a bid on time
of forgotten goals and broken ties
turn me from my shame
lay them before me, brazen like my gaze.

In hopes that I will see
And feel something beside this hole
made from my toxic stroll
towards something that's old.
And cold.

I wonder I wonder
If I can ever be the one to forget
the one to neglect the past's mischiefs
as the chief of my persona.

My actions are nothing
but its aura being reflected
as my own because I am owned.
Will I ever be known?

Brighter Days

Cloudy days are meant for rain
Rainy days to bring good fruit
Sunny days to bring back life
They are all life's teachings that the circle of life is ever spinning,
a perfect balance
from one continuum to the next.

Wish You Could See Me

If you said my name like you breathe me hate,
maybe I'd be your mate in spite of my sanity
to erase your prophecy.

I would glide and slide, building up the red sea
As a cache inside of me.
I wish you could see me now
I wish you could see me walk
past your pharaoh's mask.

I wish you could see me proud
All the while aware of your misguided tasks.
I want you to see me through the crowd;
A tall gazelle named Carpel.

In spite of all the hell
that you have built inside of me;
Here I stand well by your shadow
radiating this light that can only belong to me
knowing you did not break me.

New Year

One year came, one year gone
Hard to say what I'm feeling inside
A bit conflicted, disjointed in parts
Yet, I hold on to dear hope, my friend.
Happy new year to one and all

Who's to say what's coming
No one can know
We keep hoping and dreaming
For some, fading

Yet the years come and go
It don't need us to know
what's up ahead

It is a mystery, you see
Close your eyes or open real wide
New year coming
Happy new year to one and all.

I Am a Wanderer

I am a wanderer, hidden beneath the mask that I wear

I am a wanderer, pieces to a puzzle
Camouflaged in secret are my innermost thoughts
which no one can know

I am a wanderer traveling on high seas
rocking side to side evading life's pulls and thrusts
whispering soundly to those who can hear me,
"I am here and I see you. You are not alone."

I am a wanderer; no friend to the crowd
Spotted and dotted, a black sheep among wolves

I am a wanderer; silent but mighty
A wise guru with so much to say
yet no one to hear me

I am a wanderer who is feeling alone
My thoughts are my own but I am trapped in this stone
Blocking my exit with no place to go
Will my wandering days ever cease?

This, I sure hope.
Until then, I am a wanderer who is rare in its form.
Are you a wanderer, someone like me?

Sinking

I'm in the middle of a dark ocean
looking for something to hold on to.
Screaming, my voice echoes wearily
Sending vibrations through vast open waters

I'm sinking little by little, pleading in my plight.
There, I see the bright light coming slowly my way.
I hold my breath in anticipation
waiting to confirm if I'm dreaming or alive
or if truly what I'm seeing is my lifeguard at wait.

The light flashes, twinkling like a star
and just like that I know my plight is almost over.
A sigh of cautious relief I inhale
how sweet it is to almost be there.

Virgin

I am a virgin to a lot of things
but I am not a virgin to ignorance.
I am a product of survival,
faith,
and perseverance.

So please stop calling me names that rhyme with itch and doe
because I am not part of your foundation of unawareness.
I pray that you rise above the dissonance of the words
that you choose to express.

When I call out a rhyme, it doesn't keep company
with symphonies that recite loathing.
I will not back it up and bring it low
all the while disgracing my self-worth.

My heart is not weak because I cry
and the bags under my eyes
are not something to cut or to slice.
I am who I was made to be
and will be who I choose to be.

I am not typical. I am atypical.
I decline the notion that my hair is difficult
When I run my fingers through hair that tangles,
I thank my Creator because it reveals strength.
It links and coils like I coil with my lover's
heart, mind, and soul.

It is not a disaster because it is loud.
I do not choose to disgrace my ancestors
by calling hair like mine kinky
unless kinky means beautiful
because I am beautiful.

So please: stop.
I overcame and will continue to overcome.
I am not someone to neglect or to hurt.
I am not here to please your ego or to fit into the crowd.

I am a product of Ayiti. I am a product of prayer.
I am a product of innocence.
I am a product of hurt,
pain,
and neglect.

But what I am not, is a product of your ignorance.

Where Is Her Honor?

Her value, measured little to nothing
An item to be possessed
yet barely a creature to be fondled or caressed
with hands that show a consciousness
of her dignity and worth

She is rarely praised for giving life
to a world that labels her common.
Not even worth the adoration
of the young men and women
for whom she sacrificed her all

The months she gave up her life
to tears, scars, worries and queasy nights
mean nothing to the sons or daughters
she once cared for

A life of sacrifices she lives,
the unsung hero she is
Rejected and dejected
by sons and daughters she birthed
nestled in her bosom, nourished to strength
beings that would one day call her
unspeakable words;
derogatory and filled with spite.

Not recognizing that she is the reason
for him being,
he curses the mother that saved her last penny
to give him a bike
Not realizing her importance,
he uses others like her as mere sex ploys
viewing them worthless and weak.
Disassociating the two.
Seeing women as merely a means
to satisfy the flesh

her intelligence is diminished
by the men that she raised,
the society she gave her all

But who is she but a woman?
Not the vessel of life but one to be subjected.
So I say: woman, where is your honor?

Dreaming

I am searching for something this world does not offer
Yearning for a peace many are after

Eyes to the sky I see infinite measures
Hands reaching high
There, I'm growing much taller
Up, up I go
Dreaming above water.

Lost

Lost beings, lost minds,
seeing human knowledge as a god
yet denying the power of a human life
at the expense of higher wisdom.

Raising a future generation with no guiding light
What is a cripple but something to write off
to erase from a dangerous Utopia
created by unstable minds of societal elects.

Promoting massacres to sustain sadistic plots.
Truly, there is nothing more troubling
than pseudo intellect wrapped in human selfishness.
The greater desire to live portrayed as a reason to kill.
Oh lost race, with little value for life.

Life is more than health, riches, beauty, and fame.
It is the essence of living souls, each with a saying that goes
I am here and have something to say
I am here trying to live and love everyday

Yet, we play god and choose day after day
who lives and who dies

Not realizing that in the end, it'd be no race at all
but feeble mortal beings
with no value or understanding
for the transcendent nature of life.

Holiday Cheer

Winter chills are up ahead
prickled skin and hats to follow
Crisp cold air
Feel the breeze
Nifty boots and sweater weather
Such amusement in the air
Time for carols and a little bit of meddle
With holiday pie right in the middle!

People laughing everywhere
Lights are gleaming on the tree
Gifts are hidden right beneath
Gleeful children, such excitement
Hard to wait to see what's there

Adults are ready to mingle
with hot chocolate in hand
Hear the music in the air?
The holiday season bids you well.

Familial Pain

Ink stains on messy hearts
on account of trivial pursuits with no end in sight.

Wishing you were stronger than what you have shown yourself to be
but deep inside, I know your limitations
will likely be what I have come to know and always feared
always dreaded was true.

Small, I feel thinking about it all.
Wondering if holding on to hope is insanity or strength.

The quiet child inside of me getting louder by the day,
wanting what you are incapable to give.
Sometimes, healing must come without bandages or ice packs.
And it all has to happen from the inside out.

Deeper peace one day will come.
Maybe then the inner child will not be so loud.

Here today, gone tomorrow they say.
Nothing in life is guaranteed.
Same old lines, don't make this hurt less real.

Living life fully seeming at odds with our desire to live
and dream of a future we long for but cannot fully see.
When death's dreadful hand comes at the foot of the door,
we're left to wonder what is the meaning of it all.

To have loved and lost, desiring so much more.
Only the hope of salvation I have to pull me through this world
that is not my forever home.

Fearful

Fearful world of troubled people
Begging for a master yet rejecting a creator
Giving men applause, but sitting by the sidelines
Rebuking the brave, yet believing the ruler

Powers that be are reaping the profits
hiding in the shadows with virtuousness their guise

It's all an illusion
Blinded and shackled with permission
Unaware of the prison set for ahead
Mind broken, spirit stricken, hands tied
Nowhere to go

Where is the justice?
Where is the peace?
The few that can see watch in horror
Their faces masked evading discovery

Witnesses abounding but moving through obscurities
Children strapped at the breasts
Clinging for comfort with no exit in sight

I see the way out
I cling to the hope
That one day the light
will bind what is dark.

Woman

Woman, woman, guard your heart
Many come to steal it, use it, and abuse it
but precious it is to the one who knows it
The one who will cherish it above all else
Woman, woman, guard your heart
It's not to be played with;
guard it like treasure for the one who is worthy
Many come to bind your hands, cover your eyes
and play with your mind
but how priceless is the heart that lives within
that will care and love, laying head on lover's tender breasts
Hold the key to the magic within
because woman, woman, guard your heart
Many come to steal it, use it, and abuse it.

Windy Day

Windy day, what is your story?
Grey sky is staring down at me
Orchestrating a masterpiece,
singing full of majesty
beckoning me to come and see
Come and hear if you listen closely

Oh how I love to feel the breeze
of a windy day telling its story
of love lost or never found at all.
of triumphant adventure
or ghastly solace
found in the quiet mornings when all is asleep

Windy day, what is your story?
Come and tell it to me.
Is it tunes of love or songs of despair?
Come and whisper it to me.

Running

Left. Right. Left. Right.
My heart's beating and chest heaving
Huffing and puffing my way to the top of the hill
It hurts but this is the only way
I know how to be

Something about the pain outside of me
seems to awaken something inside of me
reminding me to be more than
the corpse that just wants to lay asleep

All day and night,
I just want to cry a shout of victory
because somewhere deep inside of me;
I know.

I know that I have to be more than this life I live
But then again, the voice inside of me goes:
Do you really want to live and push so hard?
Breathe so hard?

Go 'head and just live a life of ease
We've only got a few years on this earth
Why waste it on the pain—the fight
when we can just be?

My pace slows, my breathing calms
My legs slow down and I look at the sky.
There's got to be more out there than this
I have to keep running.

Afloat

I am floating on top of the sea
with the waves carrying me.
I sway side to side staring up at the sky.
I keep having this dream that doesn't seem to leave my mind.
It's almost like I'm living a lie.
Perhaps there's some meaning in there
that I'm too dull to decipher
But I just know,
I want to go along for the ride.

Thankful

Thankful for the strength that lies
and simmers within
The roaring lioness that rises from the deep
and is lifted high on the foundations that created me

The hips and thighs that expand to create life
The heart of survival and insurmountable love:
a mirror of battles conquered slowly

Strong and mighty
A reflection of beauty unlike any other.
Fighter. Protector. Lover and friend.

The majestic soul within us all
Uniquely weaved and preciously stored
Plant it deeply in treasured soil.

Index

A

awaken, 44

B

beauty, 4, 5, 12, 37, 47
beginning, 6, 8, 12, 15
beings, 34, 37
black, 3, 4, 11, 30
break, 28
breathe, 28
Breathe, 3, 4, 44
bright, 5, 31
buried, 1

C

child, 39
Child, 13
children, 1, 10, 17, 38
Children, 15, 41
conflicted, 23, 29
creator, 41
Creator, 32
cry, 10, 32, 44

D

dad, 1
Daddy, 15
dark, 23, 31, 41
daydreaming, 2, 17
days, 26, 27, 30
deep, 9, 39, 44, 47
Defense, 13
dream, 2, 4, 22, 39, 46

F

faces, 3, 4, 6, 11, 41
fight, 13, 14, 18, 24, 44
free, 5, 24
future, 37, 39

G

generation, 3, 4, 37
god, 37
God, 23

Index

H

hair, 32, 33
healing, 20, 39
heart, 1, 23, 32, 42, 44, 47
hearts, 20, 39
hide, 8, 23
home, 24, 40
hope, 4, 16, 29, 30, 39, 40, 41
human, 37
hurt, 33, 39
hurts, 44

I

inside, 1, 28, 29, 39, 44

L

lies, 3, 7, 26, 47
life, 1, 2, 4, 6, 17, 26, 27, 30, 34, 35, 37, 39, 44, 47
light, 2, 16, 28, 31, 37, 41
live, 22, 37, 39, 44
living, 17, 26, 37, 39, 46
lost, 37, 40, 43
love, 2, 20, 24, 37, 42, 43, 47

M

made, 2, 3, 26, 32
mask, 14, 28, 30
men, 13, 34, 35, 41
mind, 9, 12, 32, 42, 46
minds, 3, 7, 37
Momma, 15

N

nature, 5, 37
new, 15, 18, 29

P

pain, 1, 33, 44
Pain, 39
peace, 5, 20, 21, 36, 39, 41

Q

quarrel, 8, 9
quiet, 7, 39, 43

R

rising, 15, 18
ruler, 41

S

sea, 23, 28, 46
see, 3, 4, 5, 7, 10, 17, 20, 21, 23, 26, 28, 29, 30, 31, 36, 38, 39, 41, 43
shadow, 28
soul, 7, 16, 32, 47
speak, 10, 18, 23
spirit, 7, 41
storm, 10, 12
story, 43
strength, 4, 24, 32, 34, 39, 47

T

thoughts, 23, 30
trees, 5, 10

U

us, 7, 12, 13, 15, 29, 47

V

voice, 7, 18, 31, 44

Index

W

wanderer, 30
war, 13, 20
War, 17
weak, 32, 35
whisper, 43
woman, 35, 42
wonder, 25, 26, 39

words, 1, 3, 4, 21, 25, 32, 34
world, 23, 34, 36, 40, 41
worth, 21, 34

Y

youth, 3